Let's Talk Trash

The Kids' Book About Recycling

Kelly McQueen
David Fassler, M.D.

with the Environmental Law Foundation

Waterfront Books
98 Brookes Avenue
Burlington, Vermont 05401

Copyright © 1991 by Waterfront Books

All rights reserved. No part of this book may be reproduced in any form or by any means without permission in writing from the publisher.

Designed and produced by Robinson Book Associates
and Bold Face Type & Design
Printed in the United States

Distributed by The Talman Company, 150 Fifth Ave.,
New York, NY 10011

Library of Congress Cataloging-in-Publication Data

McQueen, Kelly, 1962-
    Let's talk trash: the kids' book about recycling / Kelly McQueen, David Fassler
      p.   cm.
    Includes bibliographical references.
    Summary: Discusses trash and the different ways in which it can be handled, with an emphasis on recycling. Incorporates the thoughts, questions, and drawings of children.

ISBN 0-914525-19-0 paperback $14.95
ISBN 0-914525-20-4 plastic comb spiral $18.95
    1. Refuse and refuse disposal — Juvenile literature. 2. Recycling (Waste, etc.) — Juvenile literature. [1. Refuse and refuse disposl. 2. Recycling (Waste, etc.)].
I. Fassler, David. II. Environmental Law Foundation. III. Title.
TD792.M38 1991
363.72'8–dc20   90-21400
                                                                          CIP
                                                                           AC

About This Book

Children are increasingly aware of environmental issues. They hear about oil spills, rain forests and recycling on television and in school. They learn about endangered animals at the zoo, the aquarium and the children's museum. They feel the effects of pollution when a favorite beach is closed in the summer. And children are also worried. They worry about the future of the earth. What will the world be like for their children? And their children's children?

Let's Talk Trash addresses one of the major environmental issues facing the world today. The book presents the problem of solid waste disposal in a manner designed to help children understand and explore this complex topic. *Let's Talk Trash* was written with the help of children between the ages of five and twelve. It incorporates their actual thoughts, questions, and drawings. *Let's Talk Trash* is not designed to answer all questions about solid waste disposal and recycling. Rather, it is intended to introduce the topic to young children and encourage further thought and discussion.

Kelly McQueen
David Fassler, M.D.
Burlington, Vermont

Acknowledgments

This book was made possible through the support and encouragement of the Environmental Law Foundation, an organization dedicated to enhancing education and awareness about environmental issues. We would also like to thank the following friends and colleagues for their encouragement, contributions, and constructive feedback:

Lissy Abernathy
Ryan Abernathy
Michael Bender
Carole Betts, L.Ps.
Douglas Betts, M.D.
Lucia Copeland, RN, MS
Rachel Copeland
Sara Copeland
Anna Cotton
Billy Cotton
Mary Cotton
Nancy Cotton, Ph.D.
Kim Danforth
Jimmy Duncan
Lizzy Duncan

Paula Duncan, M.D.
Ellen Fassler, MSW
Constance Fournier, Ph.D.
Erica Grayson
Sara Grayson
Vanessa Hansen-Mayer
Paul Helzer
Amanda Hemley
Mark Hemley
Marcia Hemley, Ph.D.
Marcia Jaquith
Marilynn Reed Kelly
Mike McQueen, M.D.
Alison Minkoff
Rebecca Minkoff

John Moyers
Sean Newhouse
Sue Niquette
Carrie Redlich, M.D.
Frank Reed, Ph.D.
Alicia Roberts
Amy Rofman
Julie Rofman
Paul Schwartzberg
David Slaughter, Ph.D.
Bob Stockett
Dan Talbert
Kathy Talbert
Marty Waldron

We are also grateful to the many children who shared their thoughts, questions, and creative expressions.

What is trash?

Trash is everything we throw away.

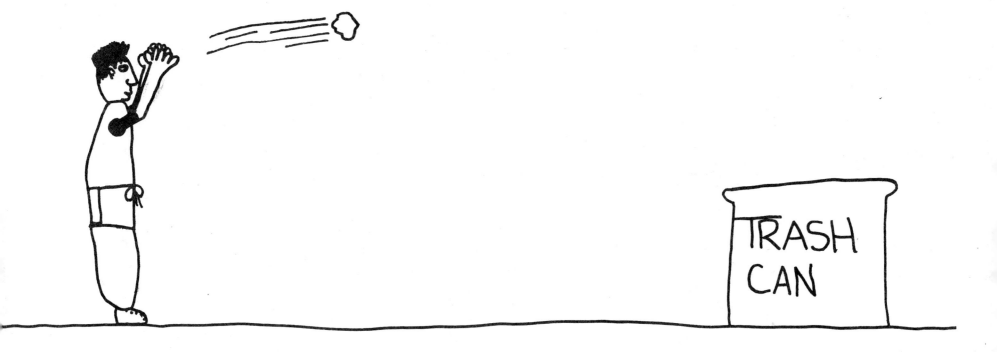

Trash is what's left after you use the part you're supposed to use.

Trash is:

newspapers	broken toys	tires
refrigerators	cans	old cars
jars	milk cartons	candy wrappers
chicken bones	cardboard boxes	leaves
bottles	tin foil	rags
leftover food	tea bags	banana peels

Can you think of other kinds of trash?

People have different words for trash.

- garbage

- waste

- junk

- debris

- refuse

- litter

- rubbish

Can you think of any other words for trash?

We call it trash when it's in the house and garbage when we take it out.

I don't like taking out the garbage.

Draw a picture of trash.

trash

Where does trash come from?

Trash comes from lots of different places.

Trash comes from:

- homes
- schools
- offices
- baseball parks
- stores

- ice skating rinks
- factories
- movie theaters
- hospitals
- gas stations

Can you think of other places trash can come from?

A lot of trash comes in the Mail.

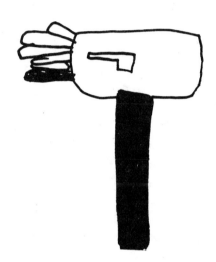

Who makes trash?

Everybody makes trash.

Moms and dads make trash.

My Dad Makes trash when he pays the bills.

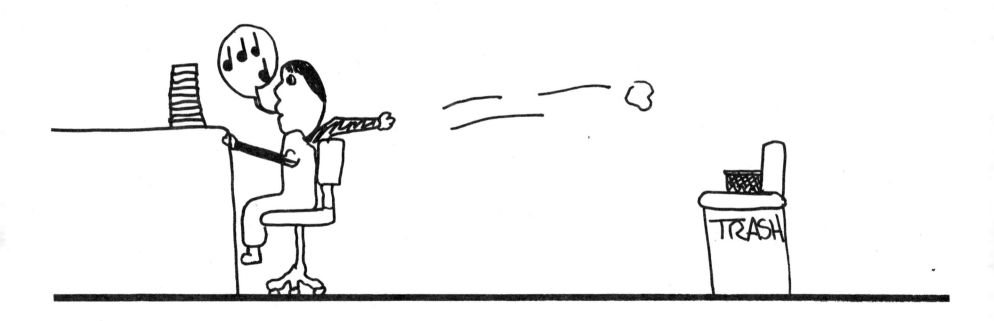

Babies make trash.

Teachers make trash.

Doctors make trash.

Kids make lots of trash, too.

Draw a picture of some of your trash.

MY TRASH

What happens to all the trash?

Lots of trash goes to a dump or landfill.

A landfill is a big hole in the ground where people put all kinds of trash.

Draw a picture of a landfill.

Some people bring their trash to the landfill.

Others send it in a truck.

What happens to the trash at the landfill?

The trash just stays in a big pile. And the pile keeps getting bigger and bigger . . .

until there's no more room. Then the landfill has to be closed.

Then what happens to the trash?

The trash just stays there . . . for a very long time.

Landfills have lots of other problems, too.

- They take up lots of room.

- They can get full.

- They cost lots of money.

- They can pollute the air, water, and soil.

Draw a picture of pollution.

Pollution

What else can we do with trash?

Some people burn their trash.

Burning trash can make it smaller, but the ashes still have to go to the landfill.

Burning trash also pollutes the air.

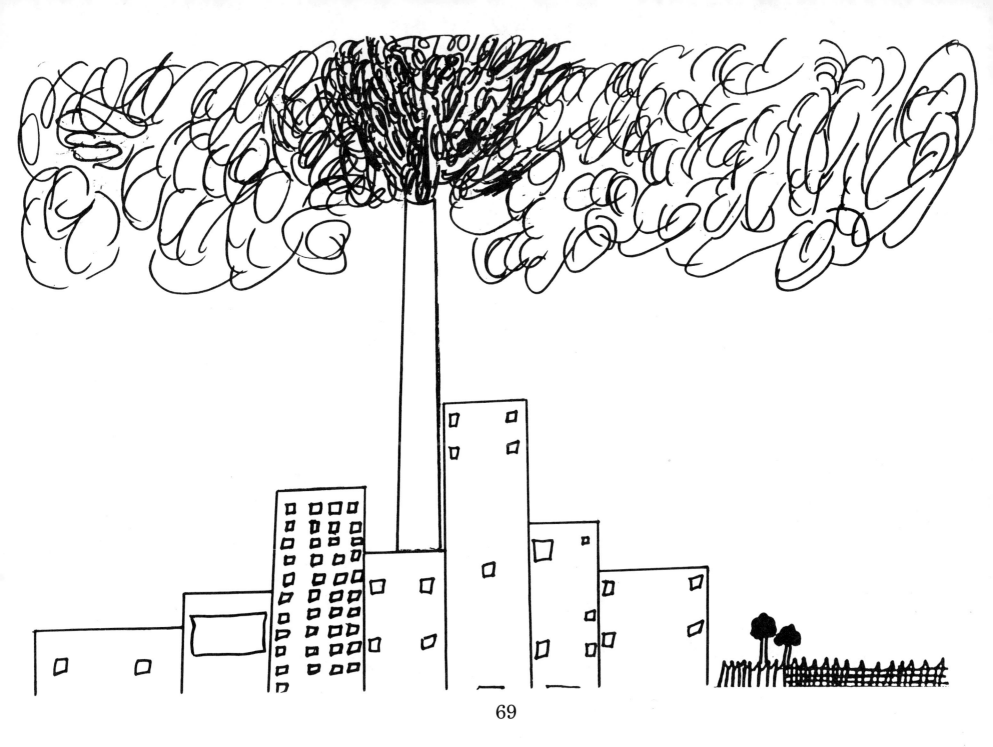

If the air gets too polluted the snow could start turning brown!

Trash is a BIG problem.

So, what <u>should</u> we do with our trash?

Maybe we could just send it to the moon.

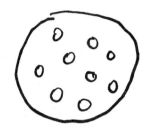

If we sent our trash to the moon it would just cause a problem there. We need to take care of our trash without making new problems.

What <u>can</u> we do about the trash problem?

There are lots of things we can do.

We can: **Reduce**

Reuse

Compost and

Recycle our trash.

There are lots of ways we can **reduce** the amount of trash we make.

We can:

- buy things without lots of extra wrapping

- keep things until they're all used up

- buy a few BIG packages instead of lots of little ones

- buy things we can refill

- take care of the things we have so they last longer

- fix things when they break instead of throwing them away

My mom gets a GIANT box of laundry soap.
It lasts a really long time.

My Dad helped me fix my wagon.

We bring our own shopping bags to the store.

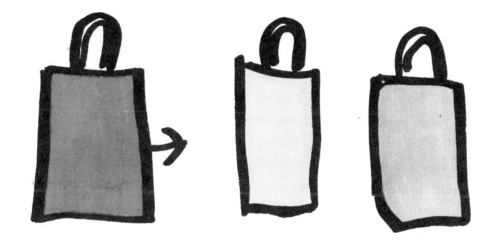

Mom refills my lunchbox

Can you think of any other ways we could make less trash?

We can also **reuse** some kinds of trash.

I give my clothes to my little brother and he wears them.

My Dad made me a swing from an old tire.

I use empty jars to keep stuff in.

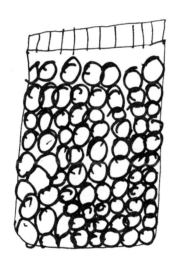  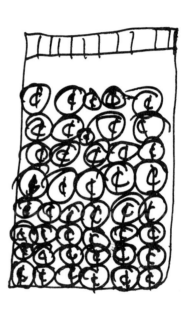

Draw a picture of a way to reuse trash.

Some kinds of trash, like leftover food and piles of leaves, can be **composted.**

Composting is when we put trash in a hole, a can, or a big pile and let it rot.

Then we can use it to help grow flowers and vegetables.

Other kinds of trash can be **recycled.**

When we **recycle** trash we change it so it can be used again.

We can **recycle** trash by:

- melting it

- grinding it

- crushing it

- shredding it

- taking it apart

- mixing it with other things

- treating it with chemicals

- smashing it up into little pieces

Then we can take what's left and use it to make new things.

You need really special machines to recycle trash.

Draw a picture of a recycling machine.

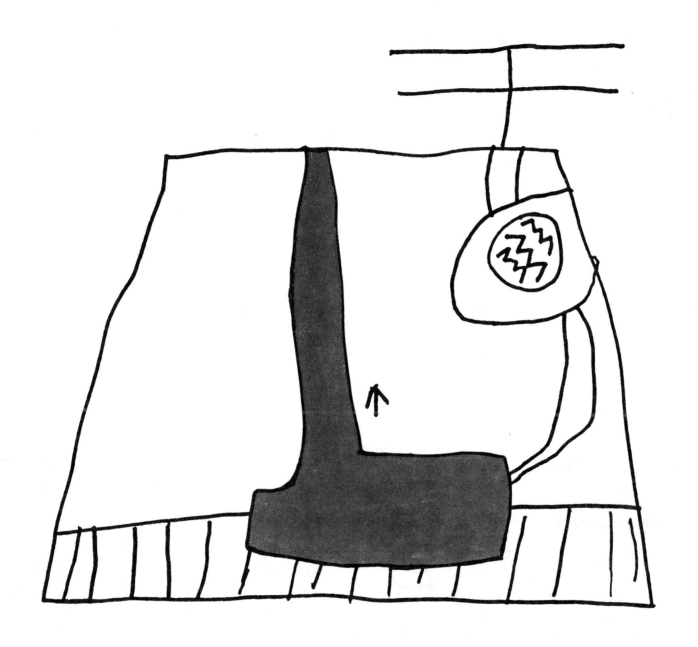

Bottle crusher

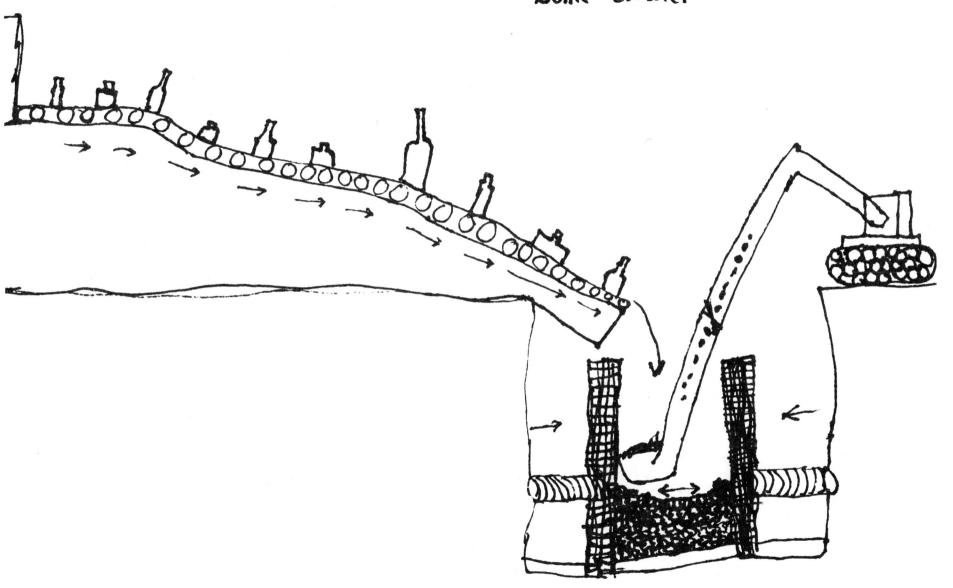

115

What kinds of trash can be recycled?

We can **recycle:**

- bottles
- jars
- newspaper
- cans
- tires
- cardboard boxes
- Christmas trees
- magazines

Some kinds of trash are harder to **recycle:**

- disposable diapers

- plastic wrap

- engine oil

- washing machines

- batteries

Draw a picture of something you can recycle.

= old clothes

= plastic bottles

or

– wood

– Newspapers

– Glass cans + bottles

– cans

Things you can recycle.

We separate our trash so it's easier to recycle.

Why should we recycle trash — isn't it a lot of work?

Recycling does take some work, but it's pretty important.

Can you think of some reasons why we should **recycle** our trash?

You can get alot of nickels.

It's fun to go to the recycling center!

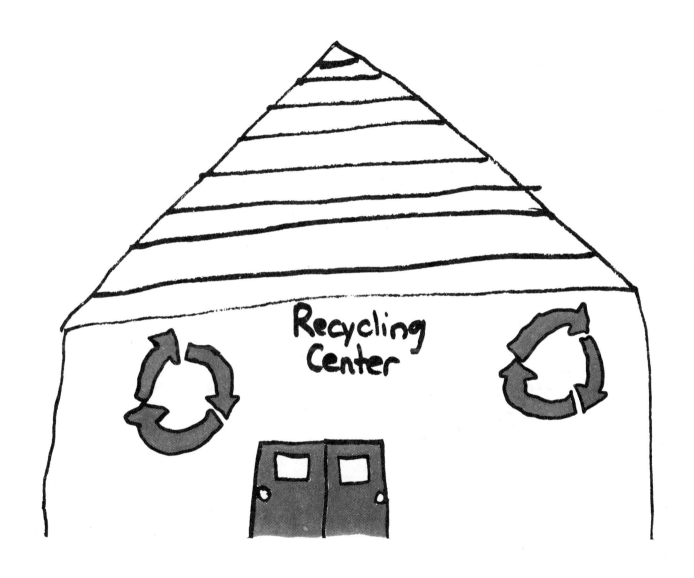

Recycling saves trees!

If we don't recycle some of our trash we might run out of places to put it all.

The whole earth covered with trash

Even with more and more people starting to **reduce, reuse, compost** and **recycle,** trash is still a BIG PROBLEM.

So, what else can we do about the trash problem?

We can think about the trash problem when we buy things.

We can think about the trash problem when we throw things away.

We can talk to our brothers, sisters, parents, teachers and friends about the trash problem.

We can all remember to:

        Reduce

        Reuse

        Compost and

        Recycle!

What questions do you have about trash?

These pages are for you to make up stories or poems or draw any pictures you want.

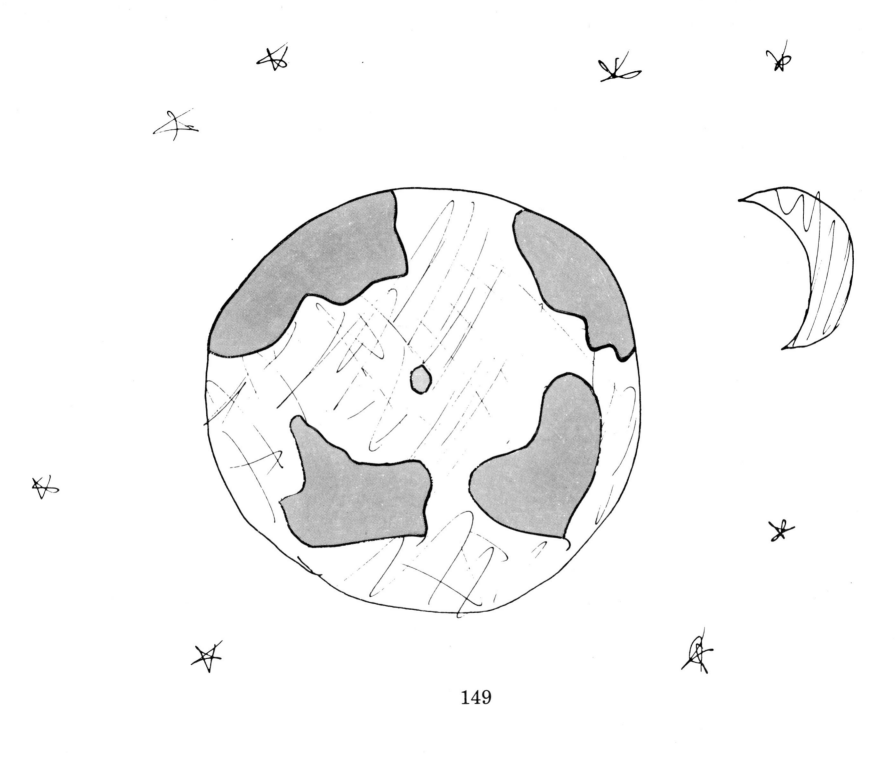

Resources

Agencies and Organizations

Center for Environmental
  Education
1725 DeSales Street, N.W.
Suite 500
Washington, DC 20036

The Environmental Law
  Foundation
26 State Street
Montpelier, VT 05602

Environmental Action
  Coalition
625 Broadway
New York, NY 10012

The Environmental Defense Fund
1616 P Street, N.W.
Suite 150
Washington, DC 20036

Coalition for Recyclable Waste
c/o Environmental Action
1525 New Hampshire Avenue, N.W.
Washington, DC 20036

Environmental Research
  Foundation
PO Box 3541
Princeton, NJ 08543

Greenpeace
1436 U Street, N.W.
Washington, DC 20009

U.S. Environmental
  Protection Agency
Office of Solid Waste
402 M Street, S.W.
Washington, DC 20460

The Aluminium Association
900 19th Street, N.W.
Washington, DC 20006

World Resources Institute
1735 New York Avenue, N.W.
Washington, DC 20006

Citizens for a Better
  Environment
PO Box 926
Arlington, VA 22216

Environmental Policy Institute
218 D Street, S.E.
Washington, DC 20036

Environmental Action
1525 New Hampshire Ave., N.W.
Washington, DC 20036

American Paper Institute
260 Madison Avenue
New York, NY 10016

Earth Island Institute
300 Broadway, Suite 28
San Francisco, CA 94133

National Association of
  Recycling Industries
330 Madison Avenue
New York, NY 10017

National Wildlife Federation
1500 16th Street, N.W.
Washington, DC 20036

National Recycling Coalition
45 Rockefeller Plaza,
  Room 2350
New York, NY 10111

Worldwatch Institute
1776 Massachusetts Ave., N.W.
Washington, DC 20036

The Kids' Earth Works Group
1400 Shattuck Avenue, #25
Berkeley, CA 94709

Council on Economic Priorities
30 Irving Place
New York, NY 10003

National Solid Wastes
  Management Association
1730 Rhode Island Avenue, N.W.
Suite 1000
Washington, DC 20036

The Natural Resource
  Defense Council
40 West 20th Street
New York, NY 10011

Renew America
1001 Connecticut Ave., N.W.
Suite 1719
Washington, DC 20036

National Center for Resource
  Recovery, Inc.
1211 Connecticut Avenue, N.W.
Washington, DC 20036

Institute for Local Self
  Reliance
2425 18th Street, N.W.
Washington, DC 20009

Center for Plastics
  Recycling Research
Rutgers University
Building 3529
Busch Campus
Piscataway, NJ 08855

Plastics Recycling Foundation
1275 K Street, N.W.
Suite 400
Washington, DC 20005

Sierra Club
PO Box 7959
San Francisco, CA 94120

Kids for a Clean Environment
PO Box 158254
Nashville, TN 37215

Companies Specializing in Recycled Products:

Earth Care Paper
P.O. Box 3335
Madison, WI 53704

Recycled Paper Company
185 Corey Road
Boston, MA 02146

Save Our Ecosystems
541 Williamette Street
Room 102
Eugene, OR 97401

Seventh Generation
Products for a Healthy Planet
55 Hercules Drive
Colchester, VT 05446

Recycled Paper Outlet
P.O. Box 10540
Portland, OR 97210

Print Power Services
3020 Allis Street
Springfield, IL 62703

Atlantic Recycled Paper Co.
PO Box 11021
Baltimore, MD 21212

LaSalle Paper
4170 Bandini Boulevard
Los Angeles, CA 90023

Acorn Designs
Box 263
5066 Mott Evans Road
Tramansburg, NY 14886

Conservatree Paper Company
10 Lombard Street
Suite 250
San Francisco, CA 94111

Vermont Important Paper Co.
P.O. Box 90
Cuttingsville, VT 05738

Sensible Supplies
322 Highland Avenue
Winchester, MA 01890

Write Now
Recycled Paper and Print
100 North Fifth Street
Lewisburg, PA 17837

Real Goods Trading Company
966 Mazzoni Street
Ukiah, CA 95482

References

Books for Kids:

Beame, R. *What Happens to Garbage?* New York: Julian Messner, 1975.

Chernoff, G. *Just a Box?* Toronto: Fitzhenry & Whiteside, 1973.

Chester, M. *Let's Go to a Recycling Center.* New York: Putnam, 1977.

Jauna, J. *50 Simple Things Kids Can Do To Save the Earth.* Kansas City: Andrews and McMeel, 1990.

Lauber, P. *Too Much Garbage.* Chicago: Garrand, 1974.

Miles, B. *Save the Earth: An Ecology Handbook for Kids.* New York: Alfred Knopf, 1974.

Seuss, Dr. *The Lorax.* New York: Random House, 1971.

Shanks, A. *About Garbage and Stuff.* New York: Viking, 1973.

Simons, R. *Recyclopedia.* Boston: Houghton Mifflin, 1976.

Wilcox, C. *Trash!* Minneapolis: Carolrhoda, 1988.

Wright, D. *Edith and the Little Bear Lend a Hand.* New York: Random House, 1972.

Books for Parents and Teachers:

Appelhoff, M. *Worms Eat My Garbage.* Kalamazoo, MI: Flower Press, 1982.

Earth Works Group. *50 Simple Things You Can Do to Save the Earth.* Berkeley: Earthworks Press, 1989.

Elkington, J., Hailes, J. and Makower, J. *The Green Consumer.* New York: Penguin Books, 1990.

Blumberg, L. and Gottlieb, R. *War on Waste.* Covelo, CA: Island Press, 1990.

Kohrell, M. *Directory of Resources: An Educator's Guide to Solid Waste Management.* Lincoln, NE: Midwest Recycling Coalition, 1987.

Let's Recycle: Lesson Suggestions for Teachers. Washington, D.C.: US EPA (publication #SW-801), 1980.

Lingelbach, J. *Hands on Nature: Information Activities for Exploring the Environment with Children.* Vermont Institute of Natural Science, 1986.

Moeger, K. *Teacher's Guide: Educational Materials in Resource Recovery.* Grades K-12. St. Paul, MN: Minnesota Pollution Control Agency, 1984.

Pringle, L. *Recycling Resources.* New York: Macmillan, 1974.

Reindl, J. *Recycling Study Guide.* Madison, WI: Wisconsin Dept. of Natural Resources, 1988.

Simons, R. *Recyclopedia: Games, Science Equipment, and Crafts from Recycled Materials.* Boston: Houghton Mifflin, 1976.

Magazines about Recycling and Environmental Issues:

Garbage
435 Ninth Street
Brooklyn, NY 11215

E Magazine
P.O. Box 5089
Westport, CT 06881

*BioCycle: The Journal of
  Waste Recycling*
33 East Minor Street
P.O. Box 351
Emmaus, PA 18049

*Conservation and Recycling:
The Management of World Wastes*
Communication Channels, Inc.
6255 Barfield Road
Atlanta, GA 30328

Recycling Today
Gie, Inc.
4012 Bridge Avenue
Cleveland, OH 44113

Waste Age
Suite 1000
1730 Rhode Island Ave., N.W.
Washington, DC 20036

Buzzworm
P.O. Box 6853
Syracuse, NY 13217

Resource Recycling:
North America's Recycling
  Journal
P.O. Box 10540
Portland, OR 97210

For Kids:

P-3
P.O. Box 52
Montgomery, VT 05470

About the Authors

David Fassler, M.D. is a child psychiatrist practicing in Burlington, Vermont. A graduate of the Yale University School of Medicine, Dr. Fassler received his training in adult psychiatry at the University of Vermont, and in child psychiatry at the Cambridge Hospital, Harvard Medical School. He is currently a clinical assistant professor and the director of continuing education in the Department of Psychiatry at the University of Vermont, and an instructor in psychiatry at Cambridge Hospital, Harvard Medical School. Dr. Fassler is also a co-author of a series of children's books dealing with family transitions and health related issues.

Kelly McQueen is a medical student at the University of Vermont. She received her undergraduate training in biology at Colorado College. Working with Dr. Fassler, Ms. McQueen co-authored *What's a Virus, Anyway?*, the first children's book designed to explain AIDS to young children.

About the Environmental Law Foundation

The Environmental Law Foundation is a non-profit organization dedicated to helping people understand and address environmental issues in their communities. The E.L.F. is not an advocacy organization. Instead, we help others understand their own legal and environmental options. We encourage people to participate in the implementation of sound environmental policies. The E.L.F. provides technical and legal information and assistance to organizations, local government, businesses, and individuals to help them:

- Preserve open space and agricultural land
- Establish sustainable recycling programs
- Manage solid and hazardous waste
- Manage and plan for growth
- Encourage environmentally sound development
- Develop educational programs about environmental issues
- Resolve environmental disputes

Membership in the E.L.F. includes parents, teachers, planners, lawyers, engineers, doctors, businesses and government agencies. For more information about the E.L.F., please write to us at 26 State Street, Montpelier, Vermont 05602.

Special Issues for Kids!

WHAT'S A VIRUS ANYWAY?
The Kids' Book About AIDS
David Fassler, M.D. and Kelly McQueen

AIDS can be a difficult subject to discuss with young children. However, children hear a lot about the disease at a very early age. *What's a Virus, Anyway?* is a simple introduction to help adults talk with children. The book includes children's drawings and questions, and provides basic information in a manner appropriate for 4-10 year olds.

"...that people with AIDS are just like everyone else, makes this book particularly distinctive." —**Booklist**

$8.95 paperback, $12.95 plastic comb spiral
Ages 4-10. 70 pages. Illustrated by children.

Also, now a new Spanish edition:
¿QUE ES UN VIRUS?
Un libro para ninos sobre el SIDA

MY KIND OF FAMILY
A Book for Kids in Single-Parent Homes
Michele Lash, A.T.R.,
Sally Ives Loughridge, Ph.D.,
and David Fassler, M.D.

Designed to help children express, explore and understand some of the special issues and feelings associated with living in a single-parent home.

$14.95 paper, $18.95 plastic comb spiral
208 pages, illustrated by children. Ages 4-12

CHANGING FAMILIES
A Guide for Kids and Grown-ups
David Fassler, M.D.; Michele Lash, A.T.R.
and Sally B. Ives, Ph.D.

This book helps children cope with the emotional confusion of being in a changing family. Divorce, remarriage, new surroundings, and new relatives are a few of the changes presented for discussion here.

"Many children of divorce openly or secretly hope that their biological parents will reunite. The new marriage shatters that illusion." —**David Fassler, "Parent & Child," New York Times**

$14.95 paper, $18.95 plastic comb spiral
192 pages, illustrated by children. Ages 4-12

LET'S TALK TRASH
The Kids' Book About Recycling
Kelly McQueen and David Fassler, M.D.

Children hear about oil spills, rain forests, and recycling on television and in school. They worry about the earth and personally feel the effects of pollution when a favorite beach is closed in the summer. *Let's Talk Trash* presents the problem of solid waste disposal for further thought and discussion among young children, their teachers or their parents.

"As a former teacher, I highly recommend this creative introduction to an important contemporary topic."
—**Constance Fornier, Ph.D., Texas A&M University**

"Never has 'talking trash' been so much fun! This book takes a refreshing look at a tough problem. I hope kids will share this book with their parents so that we all understand why it's important to protect our beautiful environment."
—**Madeleine M. Kunin, Governor of Vermont**

$14.95 paperback, $18.95 plastic comb spiral
Ages 4-10. 168 pages. Illustrated by children.

WATERFRONT BOOKS
98 Brookes Avenue, Burlington, VT 05401
Order toll-free: 1-800-639-6063

THE DIVORCE WORKBOOK
A Guide for Kids and Families
Sally B. Ives, Ph.D., David Fassler, M.D.,
and Michele Lash, A.T.R.

"The volume takes children by the hand from marriage through separation, divorce and 'legal stuff' which defines such terms as custody, child support, divorce mediation, and visitation. It also devotes considerable attention to the emotional aftermath of divorce."
—**Nadine Brozan, The Sunday New York Times**

$12.95 paper, $16.95 plastic comb spiral
160 pages, illustrated by children. Ages 4-12

JOSH
A Boy with Dyslexia
Caroline Janover
Illustrated by Edward Epstein

This is an adventure story with a section of resources and facts about learning disabilities.

"In Josh, Caroline Janover has taken me into the mind and heart of A Boy with Dyslexia. We share his fears, tragedies, and triumphs. Must reading for all families who struggle with dyslexia."
—**Mary MacCracken, educational therapist and author of Lovey, Turnabout Children, and Circle of Children**

$7.95 paper, $11.95 hardcover.
100 pages, 15 illustrations. Ages 8-12

LUKE HAS ASTHMA, TOO
Alison Rogers
Illustrated by Michael Middleton

The story shows that asthma can be managed in a calm fashion. For the more than two million families who have children with asthma, this is an important message."
—**Thomas F. Plaut, M.D., author of Children with Asthma: A Manual for Parents**

$6.95 paper.
32 pages, illustrated. Ages 3-7

PLAYFUL PERCEPTION
Choosing How to Experience Your World
Herbert L. Leff, Ph.D.

Playful Perception invites readers to break old assumptions and view the world in new ways.

$9.95 paper, $15.95 hardcover. Classroom & workshop materials available on request.

DATE DUE			

363.72　　McQueen, Kelly.
MCQ
　　　　　　Let's talk trash :
　　　　　　the kids' book about
　　　　　　recycling

VIEW ACRES MEDIA CENTER
NORTH CLACKAMAS DISTRICT #12

791842 01271 01170A 01414E　　　001